Growing B

How To Grow And Preserve Berries:

Strawberries, Raspberries, Blackberries, Blueberries, Gooseberries, Redcurrants, Blackcurrants & Whitecurrants.

Including recipes for jams and preserves.

BY

James Paris

Published By

www.deanburnpublications.com

Blog: www.planterspost.com

Copyright

***

Contents

Introduction:

Growing fruit bushes is something that adds a new dimension to any vegetable garden, and indeed I always try to include Raspberry canes especially, into any kitchen garden plan.

With a good mixed selection of these superb fruit bushes you can be assured that at the end of the summer season, not only will you have fresh delicious fresh berries to make jams and jellies; but you will also be assured of enjoying the 'fruits' of your labour throughout the long dark winters.

There is a lot of attention lately focused on the 'fresh' food we buy on a daily basis, and especially on the subject of chemical contamination through pesticides or fertilizers.

There is also the issue of GMO (Genetically Modified) crops that many farmers are now planting – and we in turn are consuming - and irradiation techniques to prolong the shelf-life especially of soft fruits.

To many people including myself, **none of these things are a good idea!** Now that these issues have been brought to light however, the move is on to become more self-sustainable and to take more control over the food that we are feeding ourselves and our families.

Thankfully this need not be difficult, and there is no need for all that 'green finger' nonsense! 'Growing your own' simply needs the application of a few basic rules – and plenty of enthusiasm!

The rewards in this case are literally the 'fruits' of your labours, as you harvest fruit berries grown by your own hands and consume delicious jams, jellies, fruit drinks and much more; whilst experiencing the personal satisfaction to be gained by growing your own food.

Some Benefits of Growing your own:
As is the case with home-grown vegetables, the benefits of growing your own berry bushes are many.

1. By growing organically, you are assured of fresh chemical free fruit.

2. It's much cheaper to grow your own berries.

3. You have the satisfaction to be gained from growing and consuming your own produce (priceless).

4. You can look forward to summer puddings, Jams, jellies, juices & pies from your very own Berry bushes.

What you will learn from this book:

1. How to grow your own Berry bushes, including which varieties to choose from.

2. How to care for your plants in order to get the best results, including pruning and feeding.

3. Making a good organic compost that will assure you of the best crop of Berries possible.

4. How to control insect and disease using organic insecticides and Companion Planting methods.

5. Simple steps to protect your Berries from birds and flying insects.

6. Harvesting and preserving your fruits for later consumption.

Planting Zone Maps:

Different plants of course grow at different times (or not at all) according to just where they are in the world. Here are a couple of zone maps to refer to when considering whether or not a plant is suitable for your area.

USA MAP:

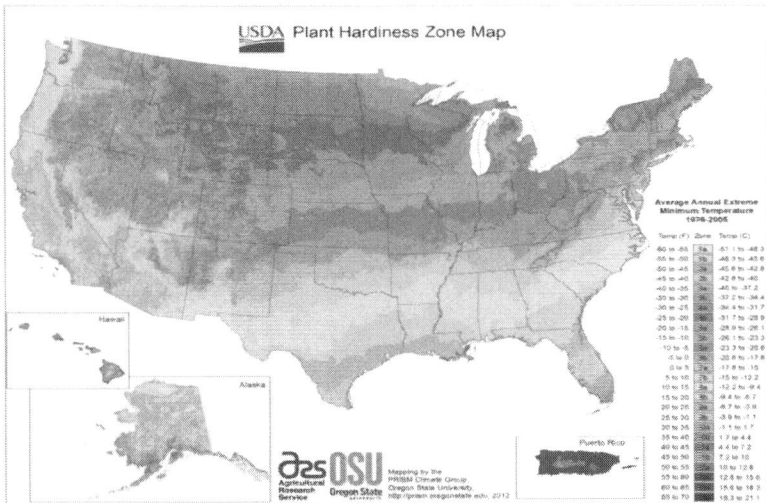

Average Annual Extreme Minimum Temperature 1976-2005

Temp (F)	Zone	Temp (C)
-60 to -55	1a	-51.1 to -48.3
-55 to -50	1b	-48.3 to -45.6
-50 to -45	2a	-45.6 to -42.8
-45 to -40	2b	-42.8 to -40
-40 to -35	3a	-40 to -37.2
-35 to -30	3b	-37.2 to -34.4
-30 to -25	4a	-34.4 to -31.7
-25 to -20	4b	-31.7 to -28.9)
-20 to -15	5a	-28.9 to -26.1 ǀ
-15 to -10	5b	-26.1 to -23.3
-10 to -5	6a	-23.3 to -20.6
-5 to 0	6b	-20.6 to -17.8
0 to 5	7a	-17.8 to -15
5 to 10	7b	-15 to -12.2
10 to 15	8a	-12.2 to -9.4
15 to 20	8b	-9.4 to -6.7
20 to 25	9a	-6.7 to -3.9
25 to 30	9b	-3.9 to -1.1
30 to 35	10a	-1.1 to 1.7
35 to 40	10b	1.7 to 4.4
40 to 45	11a	4.4 to 7.2
45 to 50	11b	7.2 to 10
50 to 55	12a	10 to 12.8
55 to 60	12b	12.8 to 15.6
60 to 65	13a	15.6 to 18.3
65 to 70	13b	18.3 to 21.1

UK MAP:

Plant Hardiness Zone Map of the British Isles

°F	Zone	°C
0 to 5	7a	-15.0 to -17.7
5 to 10	7b	-12.3 to -14.9
10 to 15	8a	-9.5 to -12.2
15 to 20	8b	-6.7 to -9.4
20 to 25	9a	-3.9 to -6.6
25 to 30	9b	-1.2 to -3.8
30 to 40	10a	1.6 to -1.1

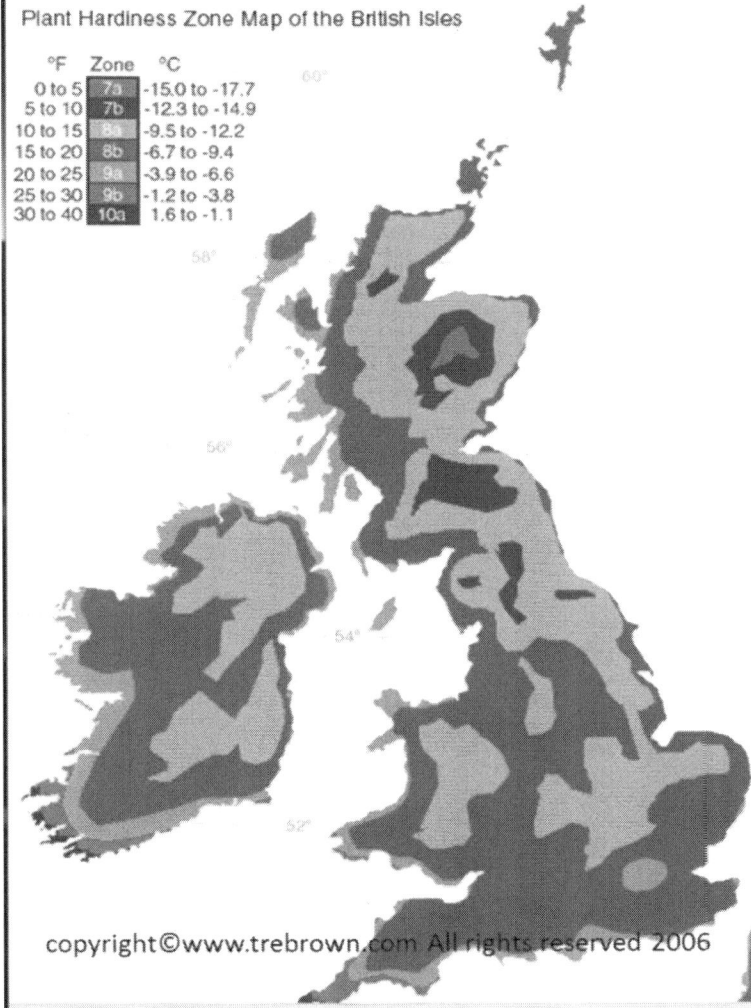

Companion Planting:

Introduction:

For those familiar with the concept of companion planting, this will indeed need no introduction and this section could skipped. However if you are unfamiliar with the idea then this brief explanation will hopefully enlighten you somewhat..

It could reasonably be claimed that Companion planting is at the 'root' (see what I did there!) of organic growing methods. This is because when it is practiced correctly then you will have no need for pesticides and artificial fertilizers.

There are both 'good' and 'bad' companions when it comes to choosing partners (plants that grow well together), and there are different ways in which they can benefit from this arrangement.

Insect Control: Controlling destructive insects is the on-going task of every gardener, and for the organic gardener it can mean reaching for the organic sprays (check out the natural remedies section), or seeking out suitable plants that will deter (or attract) specific or general insects.

Soil Nutrients: Plants can also be chosen for the nutrients that they take from, or put into the soil for the benefit of other plants. For instance legumes such as beans or peas have the ability to draw nitrogen from the air, and infuse it into the soil. This is of great benefit for those nitrogen-loving vegetables.

Protection: Plants can be chosen for their ability to shade others from the strong sun, or protect them from strong winds that they themselves can cope with but others cannot.

For a complete breakdown of Companion Planting including information on insect control and organic planting methods then please check out my book which is available on Amazon for kindle.

Pollination: Growing the correct flowering plants ensures that you attract the 'good' insects to enable pollination, and in turn assure you of abundant crops.

Companion Planting: The Vegetable Gardeners Guide. The Role of Flowers, Herbs & Organic Thinking

Throughout this book on growing berries however, I have included information on relevant companions for the different berry plants listed here.

Composting:

Excerpted from authors book on <u>Square Foot Gardening</u>

Making Good Compost

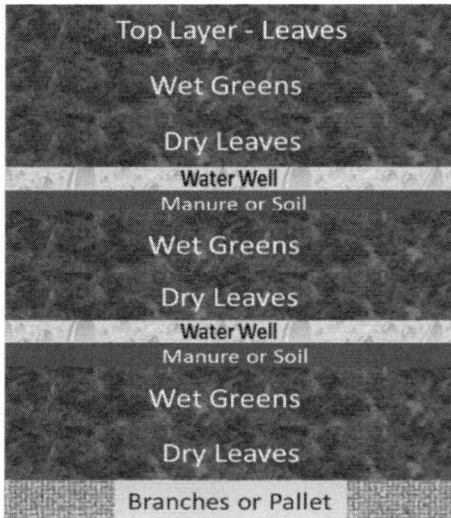

Top Layer - Leaves
Wet Greens
Dry Leaves
Water Well
Manure or Soil
Wet Greens
Dry Leaves
Water Well
Manure or Soil
Wet Greens
Dry Leaves
Branches or Pallet

If you pile up vegetable matter and let it rot over a period of time, then you will get compost. However if you want to make good compost over a shorter time then there are certain steps you have to follow.

Compost is basically formed when vegetable or organic matter is broken down by aerobic organisms. These are fungi and bacteria, which need oxygen to live. In order for the bacteria to break down the cellulose in plant matter they need nitrogen, and the more nitrogen they get the quicker they will do their job and the quicker you can achieve good compost.

Typical Compost Bin Layout

Compost Ingredients:

- **Carbon** (Dried Matter): Dried leaves, straw, wood chips, grass, small twigs.
- **Nitrogen** (fresh matter): Vegetable scraps, lawn clippings, weeds, manure.

- **Soil:** The addition of good soil adds minerals and micro-organisms to the compost, thereby stimulating aerobic composition

This layering process – including watering well between layers - generates significant heat which also kills disease organisms and weed seeds etc, in effect making it suitable for use in the garden. If there is a shortage of nitrogen then the whole process is lengthened. The job of the good compost maker is to see that this is not the case and provide suitable quantities of air, moisture and nitrogen to the mix.

With all this in mind a good composter should be constructed in such a way as to ensure good ventilation to the mix; as well as allow for turning the compost (for aeration).

Traditionally Nitrogen can be added to the mix by adding fresh dung as the nitrogen is in the urine; or by adding suitable plants such as nettles (without the roots) and grass clippings which are rich in nitrogen.

As different materials decay at different times, it is also advisable to have not just one composter, but three at least if you have the space for them. This way you can really take control over your composting efforts.

Here is a good example of home-made compost bins from pallets acquired from the local DIY store for free. The fronts of the bins are set in place in such a way that they can easily be removed for turning the compost.

Although this model will work just fine as it allows the air to circulate well; the addition of 1" chicken mesh stapled to the sides will help to keep in the compost as well as keep out unwanted vermin. With this in mind you may also want to consider a cover for your bins – though remember to water periodically to stop the compost drying out completely.

Every-Day Composting:

Whilst composting is generally carried out in a process involving turning and compost rotation, there is also what I like to call 'Every-day' compost.
This is composting in its simplest form, designed with the householder in mind who has to keep it basic and simply wants to recycle their organic waste products such as kitchen vegetable waste, as and when they have them available.

Modern composting bins like the one below are ok but are not designed to be turned over; indeed to do so would add

the new material to the old and mess up the composting process. This design therefore is intended to make a little compost at a time and the rotted material to be removed from the bottom of the bin via the access panel provided.

The fact that the dark green plastic warms up quickly helps speed up the composting process.

Composters can be made from many kinds of material, the main thing being that they allow the circulation of air and easy access for maintenance.

Positioning Compost Bins:
As for the siting of the composters themselves; the obvious answer is do not use up valuable growing space if you can avoid it. As long as your composter gets enough sunshine to warm it up slightly but not dry it out, then this will do perfectly well. Keep the bins at least 6 feet away from overhanging trees, and position where they get adequate light and a free flow of air.

How Long?
As for how long you will have to wait before you get great compost for your efforts, I'm afraid there is no definite answer! This is because of several factors that will influence the time it takes for the material to break down. The actual material itself – grass cuttings break down faster than fallen leaves for instance which can certainly take over 1 year and need a fair amount of turning.

The amount of nitrogen in the mix. Low nitrogen-rich plants or lack of manure will slow down the process. Ventilation. A well ventilated composter will work much faster than one that does not allow for an adequate flow of air.

Turning your compost regularly will increase the composting process.

Moisture content is also very important in speeding up the process. The compost should be damp like a wrung-out cloth in order to operate properly.

With all that said; in general terms rough mulching compost, ideal for setting around shrubs and bushes, or putting in the bottom of a planting hole, can usually be achieved in 3-4 months.

A smoother compost, for adding to your SFG or growing seedlings for instance, will usually take no less than 6 months to achieve – usually much longer. If conditions are not ideal then composting can take several years to achieve; making it worth that little bit extra effort to speed up the process!

Composting Materials Time-line:
Here is a short list of composting materials and the time taken to compost in ideal conditions.

Materials taking 6 months +
Kitchen vegetable trimmings (beware - stems and stalks take 2-3 years or more), annual weeds, fruit peel, lawn trimmings (no more than 15cm thick).

Material taking 1 – 2 years
Hedge clippings and prunings (except conifers and evergreens which will take more than 3 years to break down completely), paper and cardboard, autumn leaves.

Material taking 3 years +

Thick stalks and stems of plants, evergreens including holly or conifers, eggshells, sawdust & wood shavings, or thick layers of grass clippings.
Any other organic material that is large and bulky will naturally take longer to compost.

Another Option?
Finally, if you have no space to compost, or no time or whatever – consider your local authority! Many municipal authorities are composting as part of their environmental efforts, this is highly regulated and usually excellent quality – and it is often given away free or for very little cost!

If that option is not available or you would like to get started growing your vegetables immediately; then you can certainly go for store-bought compost – maybe even Mel's Mix itself, while your own composting efforts are a 'work in progress.'

Organic Insect Control

Quite apart from the Companion Planting techniques that help to control insects, there are also more 'hands on' solutions that will help to keep control of both insect and disease outbreaks amongst your plants.

Some of these simple and yet effective ideas are included in the individual sections on growing berries, however here is a more detailed breakdown of the environmentally friendly alternatives to chemical insecticides.

Pest Control Sprays:

Good for aphids greenfly, blackfly and other soft bodied sap-sucking insects. As a general rule do not spray before heavy rain forecast, and remember to spray topside and underneath the leaves of the plant.

Garlic water spray: Add one large clove of garlic peeled and chopped in half, to a 1 pint spray container and leave for 2-3 days to infuse. Spray the plant liberally to kill the bugs.

This spray also makes a fairly effective fungal treatment for your plants and will deter many other insects.

Lemon rind spray: Peel the rind from two large lemons and add to 1 pint of boiling water. Stir and leave to cool before spraying on your plants.

This is very effective against aphids and gooseberry sawfly.

Vinegar Spray: Fill your water spray bottle ¾ full with water and the rest with distilled white vinegar. This will kill aphids and larvae on contact, and other critters over a short time.

Test a small area though, at least a day before you use it on the whole plant as some plants will react badly to the acetic acid in the vinegar. If so, try diluting the mixture.

Beer Traps: This is the time-honoured way to control slugs as they just can't resist the smell of the beer – like some humans I know!

Sink a small jar into the ground slightly away from your plants and half fill with beer. The slugs will simply drown themselves in the beer. Downside is that it is a yucky job clearing them out!

Diatomaceous Earth: This is a natural product made from tiny crushed fossilised water plants. It is very effective against a number of plant predators including sawfly, coddling moth, twig borer, thrips, mites, cockroach, cutworms, slugs, snails and many other insects.

Cardboard Collars: Apply the inside of a toilet roll around the stem of your young plants in general, to protect against cutworm and slugs.

Hot Pepper spray: Chop a few hot peppers into your spray bottle and leave to infuse with water for a few days. Spray directly onto the insects.

This is a general purpose spray that is very effective against a whole range of bugs.

Be careful not to get any in your eyes though!

Horseradish Insecticide: Bring 3 quarts of water to the boil, add 2 cups of cayenne peppers, a 1 inch piece of chopped horseradish root. Add 2 cups of packed scented geranium leaves (if you have them but not essential). Let mixture steep for 1 hour, cool, strain and spray.

This is effective against Aphids, blister beetles, caterpillars, Colorado beetles, whiteflies and other soft-bodied insects.

General Propagation:

When planting your berries from the beginning, naturally you have start somewhere – and that usually includes planting from seedlings or from young plants.

However once you have berries established then getting new plants is not a problem!

There are two main ways to do this. One way is simple pruning and transplanting and the other is 'pegging' or 'layering.'

Layering:

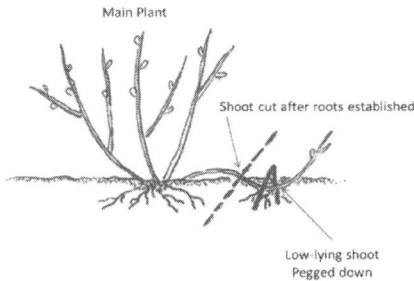

Conventional Layering is done by pegging down a trailing branch and allowing it to root as per the diagram.

Mound Layering is done as per diagram below.

Mound the earth around the main plant at the beginning of the season, or cut it back to 1 or 2 inches below the ground in the dormant season. When it grows it will send up multiple shoots from the main stem, which will be cut as per diagram and planted afresh.

Layering should be set up in the early growing season, to allow for root establishment. It may take one or two seasons for the layer to be sufficiently established for transplanting.

Earth mounded up
Encourages new growth

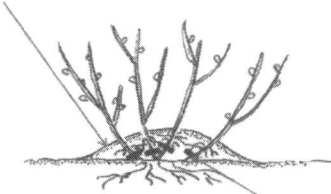

Branches are cut below ground level
after roots have been established.
Cutting transplanted elsewhere.

Cuttings:

Another way to get more plants is to simply take cuttings from good performing bushes you (or a neighbour?) already have.

For berries such as gooseberries and currant bushes, this is usually done at the end of the growing season. With raspberries & blackberries the cuttings are taken in the late summer or Autumn.

In both cases cut away 8-10 inch cuttings from a healthy-looking stem. Strip away all side shoots except the top 3, and remove any buds below the top few leaves. Push the plant down 2/3 of its length into good loamy soil; water well and leave until the spring when new growth will form.

By the end of the following season the new plants will be well established and ready for transplanting to their permanent position.

Fruit Berry Plants:

Listed below you will find a selection of the top Berry plants included in this edition. These are in no particular order, except perhaps in the popularity of the particular plant – but that of course is subject to the grower or consumer!

Strawberries, Raspberries, Blackberries, Blueberries, Gooseberries, Redcurrants, Blackcurrants & Whitecurrants

Each section is laid out in similar format to list the main points covered with respect to..

1. Planting – How to plant your berry bushes for best results.

2. Plant Care. General care of the plant including pruning tips, pest control and disease management.

3. Companions: Some good companion plants.

4. Harvesting/Preserving. How to harvest and preserve your berries for later use.

* * *

Growing Strawberries

Since the garden strawberry (*fragaria*) as we know it today, was first cultivated in France in the 1950s, it has become one of the most popular fruits available, and in used in a huge variety of products from food-related (milk shakes, ice-creams, jams, jellies, pies, coloring,) to non-food related (color, scent).

This most versatile of fruits can be successfully grown in a variety of ways including Raised Beds, containers of many kinds, hanging baskets and of course traditional garden beds.

Strawberries are hardy perennials, and although they will die back over the winter, they will quickly come back when the soil starts to warm in the spring.

Planting:
Strawberries are normally grown from runners taken as cuttings from mature plants, and are usually purchased as bare root plants or in 'plugs.'

If planting new strawberries from zone 6 northwards, then they are best planted in the early spring after the last frosts. This will ensure that they have good root growth by the following winter.

From zone 7 and southwards they can be planted in the fall. In places such as Florida they can even be grown as a winter annual.

Strawberries need to be grown in full sun and prefer a slightly acidic soil of between 5.5 and 6.5 pH. They prefer a good loamy compost with plenty of well-rotted manure and good drainage.

As the plants love to spread, plant them about 18 inches apart; making sure to cover the root area but leave the bud exposed to the sunlight. Simply press gently into the soil and water well.

Strawberry plants are often planted through a porous weed barrier laid out over the planting area. This will stop weeds and also prevent the soft fruit from laying in the wet soil.

Popular Varieties include:
Allstar – This plant produces a good crop of sweet large berries in the late spring or early summer. This is a good crop if you want all your strawberries to be ready at around the same time – for instance for freezing or jam-making.

Eversweet – This plant produces an abundance of fruit through-out the growing season, but especially late spring to early summer. Will tolerate temperatures up to 100 degrees F with no ill effects.

Quinault Strawberry – A large juicy fruit ideal for those summer sweet dishes, a favourite for strawberries and ice cream! Produces fruit from late spring right through to the late Autumn.

Plant Care:

Strawberries are fairly 'care-free' plants, and will grow enthusiastically as long as the conditions are right. In fact one of the problems can be this enthusiasm for life, as they will quickly take over an area that is not tended.

To increase fruit yield, snip away the runners and leave the fruits to grow on the plant itself. Alternatively peg down the runner until it forms roots then transplant to another area.

If the strawberries are planted on the bare soil, then cover with mulch or straw in order to keep the berries off the wet ground.

Main Predators:

Slugs are public enemy no 1 when it comes to any soft fruits – but strawberries in particular seem to whet their appetite!
Keep them at bay by laying out beer traps (refer to organic pest control section), copper barriers or Diatomaceous earth (DE) – This latter must be of the untreated variety for garden use and can be extremely effective.
Hand picking, although maybe high on the yuk! Scale, is also extremely effective. Pick the slugs when you see them and drop into a pail of salty water to kill them.

Many birds especially blackbirds love strawberries and other fruits, and so your plants will have to be protected. A simple wooden frame with plastic garden mesh stretched over it, will allow pollinating insects access while keeping out the birds.

Make sure the mesh is away from the nearest fruits, otherwise those little beaks will find their way in!

Companions:

Good companion for strawberries include the popular herb Borage. This is planted next to strawberries to increase the flavour and to encourage pollinating insects as well as insects such as wasps that will prey on destructive plant insects.

Beans and peas as well as lupin, will fix nitrogen into the soil thereby encouraging growth; whilst the lupin will attract pollinating honey bees and other beneficial insects.

Bad companions include tomatoes, potatoes and peppers as they are all prone to the same diseases. Also strawberries should not be planted next to Brassicas such as broccoli, cauliflower, Brussels sprouts, cabbage; as their growth will likely be impaired by close proximity to strawberries.

Harvesting/Preserving:

Jams & Jellies: This is the time-honoured way to preserve most fruits – check out the 'Jam Section' for recipes on jam and jelly making.

Freezing: After picking the strawberries and checking for any blemishes, wash and cut the tops off carefully and dry completely before placing in a plastic container. They will keep for about two months but will be a little soft spongy when thawed.

Freezing 2: After choosing the best strawberries, wash and dry as per prior instructions. Cut in half and place in a container with a sugar water consisting of 1 part sugar to 4 parts water. Make sure strawberries are covered and freeze. They will last around 6 months preserved in this way.

Fridge: When storing in a fridge, leave in an open container and do not wash until about to be used. Alternatively wash but be sure they are dried properly before placing in the fridge. Fruits will last around 1 week.

Growing Raspberries:

Although the Red Raspberry (*Rubus idaeus*) is the most commonly known amongst gardeners and consumers, there are now many hybrid's that come in a number of colors including, black, purple, yellow and blue!

This is an excellent plant for the Northern climates especially, and can be grown in hardiness **zones 3-9**. It is important however that you choose the proper cultivar for your area. Boyne', 'Nova', and 'Nordic' are hardy cultivars that do well in Northern regions, whilst Dorman Red', 'Bababerry', and 'Southland' will tolerate Southern warmer dryer conditions.

As a perennial plant, the raspberry cane can produce excellent fruit for many years with proper cultivation and regular pruning.

Planting:

Raspberries are best grown from certified disease-free plants, either bare-root or in containers. If you have the space, then choose a summer fruit and autumn fruit to be sure you get raspberries throughout the growing season.

Plants should be planted about two feet apart in rows also about 18 inches to two feet apart, and given extra support.

Raspberries canes will grow to 3-4 foot high.

They can also be grown against a wall or fence and supported by wire or string.

Raspberries like well manured slightly acidic soil, and they can tolerate fairly damp conditions and partial (ever-bearing varieties) to full sunshine for a good 6-8 hours per day.

Popular varieties include for example an early-ripening, red summer raspberry such as 'Algonquin' mixed with an Autumn 'Bristol' would be ideal.

You could also plant ever-bearers (Rubus idaeus 'everbearing') 'Autumn Bliss' and 'Heritage' which are ideal for beginners and will supply fruit throughout the summer and fall.

Other popular varieties include 'Canby' 'Heritage' and 'Fallgold.'

Plant Care:
One of the main areas of plant care with regard to raspberries is pruning, and if done properly this will ensure high yields and a good crop of fruits for many years.

After the first crop of fruits and at the end of the growing season, ever-bearers can simply be cut down to the ground and left to grow for the next season. Other summer fruit varieties are pruned by snipping away the depleted fruit-bearing canes, and leaving the newer canes to produce fruit for the next season.

Black and purple raspberries produce fruit from side branches grown from the main cane. During summer cut away the main canes after they have fruited, but snip the tops of new canes at about 3 foot tall to encourage side growth throughout the growing season.

Pests to look out for include Gooseberry sawfly, which is the larva of the sawfly resembling a tiny caterpillar that can strip the leaves off your plant almost overnight! This particular pest attacks raspberries, gooseberries, red and whitecurrant bushes during late spring and summer.

Spray with Nemasys 'Grow Your Own' which is a pathogenic nematode that introduces nematodes (microscopic worms) that kill a range of insects including cutworms, sawflies, carrot root fly, coddling moth.

Aphids, blackfly and greenfly are also fond of berry bushes and increase the chance of disease and fungal infection. Spray with a lemon solution made by grating the rind of a large lemon and adding to a pint of boiling water. Leave overnight and spray on the infected plant to kill the aphids.

Rasps are also prone to several fungal diseases especially in times of wet humid weather. Ensure crop has adequate air flow through the plants, and cut away and burn infected leaves.

Companions:
Good companions for raspberries include Garlic, which acts as a natural fungicide as well as discouraging beetles; and Turnip which deters the Harlequin beetle.

Planting a row of beans or peas nearby will add valuable nitrogen to the soil.

Bad companions include blackberries (not to be planted near red raspberries), potatoes and tomatoes as they are likely to carry the same diseases causing cross-contamination.

Harvesting/Preserving:
Making jams and jellies of course is a fantastic way to preserve any fruit – check out the recipes in later chapters.

Pick the raspberries on a dry day, when they should leave the plant without much effort. Keep in a fridge for up to 5 days and if making preserves like jams, choose raspberries picked fresh from the plant.

Rasps can also be frozen by spreading out on a baking tray and freezing individually in this way. After they have frozen then place into a poly bag or plastic tub and put back into freezer. This will ensure rasps do not all stick together into one large mass!

Growing Blackberries:

The blackberry, or bramble (*Rubus fruticosus*) is perhaps one of the easiest of fruit berries to grow, and indeed will soon take over the fruit patch if you allow it. This is particularly the case with the **trailing blackberry** which produces vigorous primocanes (first year growth) from the crown of the plant rather than the roots.

It does however produce plentiful sweet fruits with a unique intense flavor that make excellent jam! It will grow well in zones 3-10 but is not a hardy plant and does prefer full sunshine.

Planting:

Blackberries prefer fertile soil with good drainage and plenty of manure and organic material mixed through the growing medium. Mulching around the plants will prevent drying-out and also restrict the growth of weeds.

Be sure to plant away from any wild varieties as they are likely to infect your plants with viruses; and be sure to buy good quality virus-free plants from the nursery.

Trailing and Semi-erect cultivars (which are thorn-less) should be placed around 5 feet apart, whilst erect varieties should be around 3 feet apart. Rows should be placed around 6-8 feet apart, or closer if the technique in the picture below is followed for double rows.

Ideal planting time for bare-root plants is November-December, or as late as march for potted plants.

Plant Care:

Trailing Blackberries – just like the semi-erect varieties - are vigorous growers and will need support. This can be a wall or fence or wire strung between two well-anchored posts. Fix the wire about 18 inches apart, with the top wire set at about five feet high. After the first years growth you should have fruiting floricanes trained along the top wires, with the new primocanes on the wires below.

This can be done with a simple post sunk into the ground at the end of the rows between the plants, with a cross bar to form a 'T' on the top and another half way down. Wire or heavy string can then be fixed between them, and the plants tied to them as they grow.

When the fruiting season is finished then the old floricanes can be removed or laid on the ground where they can be mulched up in the spring – at which time the previous year's primocanes (now the floricanes) should be trained along the top wires.

Erect cultivars grow up from the crown and root suckering. They are best supported by an A-frame or similar, set at about 4 feet high. Prune the primocanes regularly by about 3 inches at about this high to promote sideways growth; this will produce a 'hedgerow' effect. In winter remove the old fruiting floricanes, and prune back the lateral branches to about 18 inches.

Popular varieties include the **'Loch Ness' AGM:** which is perhaps One of the most widely grown cultivars. This is a thornless variety that produces large sweet berries that ripen from the late summer onwards.

The **'Silvan' (Silvanberry)** This is a prolific grower, and extremely thorny! However it does produce delicious full-flavoured fruit from mid to late summer.

Other thornless semi-erect varieties include **Triple Crown and Chester Thornless.**

Pests to watch out for include of course birds – which love the fresh fruits; however they are mainly a problem for the early summer varieties. The only real protection here is to erect a frame over your plants and cover with nylon bird-netting.

Raspberry borers and fruit worm, which can cause severe damage. The borer is a small black beetle with yellow stripes that bores into the stem of the leaves to lay its eggs. The hatching larvae bore their way down to the roots and destroy the plant. Remedy is to inspect regularly for damage and to remove and burn (not compost) infected canes.

Applying Bt or *Bacillus Thuringiensis* which is a natural bacteria, makes a good biological pesticide that will control fruit worm and other larvae. Mix with water as per the instructions and spray your plants thoroughly.

Blackberry cane spot: Causes a grey spotting effect on infected plants that will occasionally spread to the leaves. Eventually this will cause the canes to split and die First signs are wilting plants and a grey spotting on affected canes, which sometimes spreads to foliage. As spots enlarge, canes may split and eventually die.

Keep a careful watch on your plants and at the first sign then cut away the infected shoots at ground level.

Companions:

Beans and peas will add valuable nutrients to the soil when planted near your blackberries. When the legumes die off at the end of the season then clip at the base rather than disturb the soil, and scatter the remains to decompose and be absorbed into the soil around the blackberry plants.

Planting Garlic between blackberry rows will help against aphids, beetles and borers – as will chives and marigolds.

The herb Tansy which produces a yellow flower, is reputed to be especially effective when planted next to plants of many kinds, as it produces a potent mix of camphor, borneol and thujone; which will repel and even kill many leaf-eating insects.

Harvesting/Preserving:

Blackberries can easily be pulled from the plant when ripe, leaving the white center-piece still on the plant. This should be done very carefully on the thorn varieties, as the thorns are quite lethal! Best to use thin plastic gloves if you do not want purple stained fingers from the juice.

Once picked they can be preserved by making a delicious jam (recipes in following chapters) or frozen separately on a flat dish, then put together in a poly bag or container before added back to the freezer.

They can also be kept in a fridge for 5 days or so, but make sure they are quite dry before storing in this way.

Growing Blueberries:

The **American Blueberry** (*Vaccinium*) is a perennial flowering plant that produces delicious indigo-colored berries when ripe, that are packed with Vitamin C, B Complex, Vitamin E, Vitamin A, Copper, Selenium, Zinc, and Iron.

There are three types of blueberries to choose from – low-bush, high-bush and hybrid half-high. Most people concentrate of the high-bush as it has many varieties to choose from, and as a result can grow in many different environments.

An excellent berry for jams, jellies and fruit sauces to pour over ice-cream! They also contain more cancer-fighting antioxidants than any other fruit or vegetable.

This plant can be grown successfully in **zones 3-7**.

Planting:

Blueberries prefer an acidic soil with plenty of organic material and a **pH between 4 and 5.5** This can be achieved by the addition of sulphur spread about 6 inches deep around the growing area of the plant. Alternatively add a good mix of conifer pines to the compost to increase acidity.

Blueberries are best bought as 1-3 year old bushes from the nursery, and planted in a good compost about 15 inches deep and wide enough to accept the root system without crushing.

Low bush varieties should be planted 2-3 feet apart, whereas high-bush varieties need to be planted around 6 feet apart. Both should be planted in late November – December if bare root, or early spring if potted.

Plant Care:
Mulch around the plant with sawdust, pine-needles or wood chippings, and water with 2 inches of water per week, especially as the fruits are developing.

Pruning. For the first 3-4 years your plants will not require pruning. After this time however a light pruning will help encourage new growth and stimulate the plant. This should be done in late winter before new growth begins again in the spring.

Low-bush varieties should be pruned by cutting back all stems right back to the ground level, while **high-bush** varieties should only have the old or dead wood pruned back, and trailing stems removed. New growth will not bear fruit until the following year, and even then will benefit from having the first blooms nipped off so that the plant will produce a better crop in the following year.

Recommended **high-bush varieties** able to withstand cold winters include 'Bluecrop', 'Blueray', 'Herbert', 'Jersey', 'Ivanhoe' 'Pioneer' or 'Meader' whilst **low-bush varieties**

– normally supplied by nurseries and unnamed - are advised for colder overall climates.

Blueberry pests include the birds which love blueberries as much as we do. The only real deterrent being to protect them with a frame covered in nylon bird-netting, as in a netted cage. Alternatively you can simply drop the netting over the bush, however you will find that the birds will get the berries nearest the netting.

Destructive insects to watch out for include the blueberry tip borer, cherry fruit-worm, and cranberry fruit worm. A home-made spray made by adding 1 or 2 garlic cloves cut in half to water in a spray bottle, will kill most soft bodied insects and grubs – it also acts as a great fungicide.

Fungal diseases which can be particularly bothersome can often be avoided by removing debris and leaf litter, and ensuring adequate air flow around the plants. Replace mulch annually to avoid any build-up of fungal spores. Spray with an organic/biological fungicide if problem persists.

Companions:
As blueberries are acid-loving plants, companions for them must be able to tolerate the same conditions. Strawberries make good companions as they are good ground cover to keep the soil around the blueberry moist, as well as a good fruit to compliment the berries!

Sacrificial plants such as nasturtium can be planted nearby to distract flying pests such as aphids & greenfly.

Harvesting/Preserving:

When blueberries are ripe for the picking, they will be dark blue in color and fall off the plant at the slightest touch. They should be slightly soft when pressed between thumb and forefinger, any hard berries will be bitter to the taste and is usually an indication that a little longer on the plant is needed.

Blueberries are much in demand for jams, preserves, pies, cakes and fruit sauces. They do not have a long shelf-life after they are picked, but will last up to 14 days if stored dry in a cool place.

To freeze them simply remove any damaged or bruised berries, wash and dry carefully then scatter in a flat dish to freeze individually. When they have frozen completely then pour into polythene freezer bags. Use within 6 months for best flavours.

For jam recipes follow instructions in later chapters.

Growing Gooseberries:

Gooseberries are deciduous shrubs and are perhaps one of the easier berry fruits to grow in that they can tolerate a wide range of soil conditions, and are a fairly hardy plant able to withstand quite severe weather conditions. The average mature plant will produce between 8 and 10 pounds of fruit.

The desert varieties make excellent eating straight from the plant when ripe, and they come in four colors, red, white, green and yellow. An excellent plant for container gardening purposes, the gooseberry is one of the 'kitchen garden' essentials.

Planting:
Some choice varieties to consider would be..
Green: Careless, Invicta
Red: Pax, Whinham's Industry
Yellow: Golden Drop, Bedford Yellow
White: Langley Gage

Although able to grow in a wide range of soils, the gooseberry plant will prosper in good well drained compost, with plenty of organic material and manure. Can be grown in **planting zones between 3-7.**

The gooseberry bush is self-supporting and so does not need a frame or other support, unless growing in fans against a wall or framework.

Bare-root plants should be planted in November or December as long as the ground is not frozen or water-logged. Container grown plants can be planted at any time.

When planting, dig a hole about 1 foot deep and 2 feet around, then place your plant and fill around with a good organic compost as mentioned. Firm around the bush and water thoroughly. Plants should be spaced around 4-5 feet apart.

Pruning should be done in the late autumn by cutting back new growth to the first 2 buds, and the leaders to about 1/3 size. Cut away any dead or damaged branches to open the center of the bush and allow for new growth.

Plant Care:
The biggest threat to the gooseberry (apart from hungry birds!), is usually the gooseberry sawfly. As mentioned in earlier chapters, this can strip the leaves from your plants virtually over-night.
Easy to spot, as they are tiny caterpillars that munch away at the leaves of the plant. Follow the instructions for controlling these pests and fungus diseases in the raspberry section, or try the garlic solution method in the previous section on blueberries.

A 'tea' (solution made from adding chives to water) of chives sprayed on the plants, will protect against downy or powdery mildew.

Companions:

Best companions for gooseberries include tomatoes and green beans, while garlic or chives can be grown to distract aphids and other destructive insects.

Plant nasturtiums as sacrificial plants to attract aphids and greenfly.

Harvesting/Preserving:

Gooseberries make excellent jams, jellies and conserves. Check out the 'jams & jellies' section.

To store fresh for up to 3 weeks, carefully wash & dry the berries on an absorbent cloth. Remove the stalk and blossom ends, then cover and store in the fridge.

To freeze follow the previous instructions but after cleaning place the berries on a flat sheet and place in the freezer. Remove when frozen solid and pour into plastic freezer bags. They can last frozen for up to 2 years.

Growing Redcurrants:

The Redcurrant (*Ribes rubrum*) is a member of the gooseberry family, and though not as popular amongst growers as the blackcurrant, and although not as popular amongst the jam-makers owing to its tart flavour; it is valued very much by chefs as a condiment and is served traditionally alongside lamb dishes.

With the berries packed with vitamin C and anti-oxidants, it means that the redcurrant bush is well worth cultivating, and can certainly make a valuable contribution to the fruit larder.

One redcurrant bush will typically produce around 8-10 lbs of fruit throughout the growing season.

Planting:

Redcurrants prefer slightly cooler regions, but can be planted in **zones 3-8**. They are completely self-fertile so one bush will thrive perfectly well without the need for cross-pollination.

They are usually purchased as cuttings from the nursery, or indeed as container grown plants, and should be planted in well manured soil or compost mix with plenty of organic material and free-draining capabilities. A **soil pH of between 6-7** is preferable for best results.

They prefer full sunshine except in the hottest climates, where partial shade and early morning sunshine is best.

Plants should be planted 3-4 feet apart and if in rows then 4-5 feet between the rows. Planting bare-root plants should take place about November to February. Sink the plant into a hole big enough to take the root system without crushing, water thoroughly and cover the crown by about two inches. Press firmly around the plant to secure.

Pot grown plants can really be planted any time, but will prosper better if planted in the Autumn or winter.

Mulching around the plant with straw or other organic material will reduce moisture loss, and also add to the nutrients. Redcurrants, as in most of the berry bushes, grow quite well in pots and make great ornamental plants on any patio.

Popular varieties include Rovada, Laxton's No. 1, Junifer and also Red Lake.

Plant Care:
As with all fruit berries, keeping the birds at bay has to be done by covering with a frame-work and nylon bird-netting – unless of course your aim is just to attract birds into the garden?

Gooseberry sawfly, aphids including blackfly and greenfly can really infest a berry plant, and so spraying with an organic insect repellent as suggested in the gooseberry sections, is recommended.

In the case of the gooseberry sawfly, picking off the creatures and destroying them is recommended in addition to spraying in cases of severe infestation.

They are also prone to mould and fungus if not properly situated where there is a good flow of air around the bush. Spray with the garlic water to help prevent this, and clear away anything that may be preventing adequate ventilation.

Bearing in mind that redcurrants produce the fruit from old wood; pruning should be done by removing very old or diseased branches in the winter, leaving the healthy previous-years growth to produce fruit in the growing season.

As the plant grows over the early summer then prune new growth back to about two buds from the main stem to keep plants compact.

Companions:
Good companions for redcurrants include garlic or chives to deter predator insects; legumes such as peas or beans will add nutrients to the soil, while strawberries will grow well in the mulch around the base and keep the area moist.

Planting marigold, honeysuckle or cornflowers nearby will encourage hoverfly whose larva feed on aphids.

Harvesting/Preserving:

Berries should be harvested by snipping away the trusses from the main stem when they are ripe and not too firm to the touch.

They can be kept for a few days in the fridge or frozen in bags still on the trusses.

Like all fruits redcurrants do of course make excellent jams and preserves (recipes in later chapters), and can be crushed to make redcurrant sauce.

Redcurrants can also be delicious dried, making a great addition to cakes & such. Blanch the currants first then it is best to use a dehydrator to dry properly as they will take ages to dry completely.

Growing Blackcurrants:

The perennial Blackcurrant (*Ribes nigrum*) is without doubt the most popular of the currant fruit plants. Its deep purple/black berries are rich in vitamin C and anti-oxidants, and its rich dye from the fruits make excellent food coloring on a domestic and commercial basis.

With the blackcurrant widely used for jams, jellies, pies, fruit drinks and a host of other food-related products; it is guaranteed to remain top of the list for kitchen garden fruit producers.

The plant itself, which is a medium sized shrub, is easy to grow in zones 3-8 in with a well-manured soil/compost of around pH 6. A healthy plant will produce around 10-12 lbs of berries.

Planting:
Blackcurrants can grow in a wide variety of soils, but prefer well drained, wet (not water-logged) loamy compost. Plenty of well-rotted manure and organic material will provide the plant with the nitrogen, phosphorous and potassium it needs to produce a bumper crop of berries.

Planting is usually done with two year old shrubs – although 1 year cuttings will still bear fruit - bare root or potted, as fruits will be harvested from these plants in the growing season. Plant 4-5 feet apart in rows divided by 6-8 feet. Follow directions as per the redcurrants.

Unlike red or Whitecurrants which fruit on old wood; blackcurrants fruit on new wood. This means that for established plants the previous year's wood should be cut to about 1/3 its length, with any old or diseased growth cut out entirely..

New plants should be pruned by cutting all shoots back to two buds above ground level. This allows the root system to get more established and produces a healthier crop in the long term.

Established plants should have the main shoots cut back by about 1/3 each year, to prevent overcrowding which will increase the chances of fungal diseases. Shoots growing out sideways should be cut back or supported to prevent fruit from lying on the ground as the shoot becomes fruit-bearing.

Cuttings taken from established plants in November can be cut to about ten inches long and heeled in over winter. These cuttings can then be planted in march to form a new bush.

Plant Care:
Plants are cared for in pretty much the same way as the redcurrant bushes, with especial attention given to keeping wild birds at bay.

Blackberries are prone to the sawfly and aphid attack in the same way as other berry plants – treatment therefore is the same as mentioned earlier.

'Big Bud' is a particular pest (blackcurrant big bud mite) that attacks the blackberry bush, resulting in enlarged buds infested by mites. These buds should be picked off and burned. Try the garlic spray or a spray made from the rind of lemon boiled in water. The bush should be inspected after fruiting, and if the problem has persisted then it is best to replace the whole bush. Burn – do not compost – the infected bush.

American gooseberry mildew can be a problem especially in a poorly ventilated area or during heavy humid weather. Try and improve ventilation if possible, and spray with the garlic water.

Keep the area around the base of the plant well mulched for moistness and nutrition.

Companions:
Good companions for blackcurrants are similar to the redcurrant variety.

Harvesting/Preserving:
Since blackcurrants have to be pruned severely at the end of the growing season anyway, many people harvest by simply cutting away complete branches and taking them indoors to remove the berries. However you do it the end result is the same and the berries have to be picked from the bunches when eating fresh.

For freezing, they can be left in small bunches and placed into freezer bags – after washing and carefully air-drying the bunch to get rid of any excess water.

Jams & juices are especially popular for the blackcurrant, and recipes can be found in following chapters.

Blackcurrants can also be made into a rather excellent wine!

Growing Whitecurrants

The Whitecurrant (*Ribes rubrum*) is a deciduous shrub growing to around 3 foot tall. Though not as popular as their cousins the red and blackcurrants, they are nevertheless delicious with a tart/sweet flavour. They are also a good source of vitamins B1 and C, and are rich in iron, copper and manganese.

Although you will get a better fruit crop with a bush, if you are short of space then a single or multi stem cordon whitecurrant can be successfully grown in a large container.

Planting:
Planting whitecurrants is exactly the same as for the other current varieties, as they all more-or-less share the same preferences with regard to pH, soil types and general growing conditions.

For some unfathomable reason these berries are not widely sold in the nurseries, so you may have to go to an online supplier - or hunt down a neighbour for some cuttings!

Popular varieties include: 'Versailles Blanche' with a large, yellow to white sweet-tasting fruit.
'White Grape' AGM: This fruit is loaded with flavour and the plant has a good strong vertical growth pattern.

'Blanka': A tasty light fruit and a high-yield plant.

Plant Care:
Whitecurrants should be treated and pruned as per the instructions for the redcurrant variety. Both of these berry plants produce fruit from the old wood, whereby the blackcurrant produces fruit from the new growth – resulting in a different pruning regime.

If planting in containers, then make sure to raise them up over the winter to enable the water to drain from the drain holes on the underside.

Gooseberry sawfly and the other predations that affect the redcurrant in particular, represent the same pests and diseases that will affect the whitecurrant. The treatment therefore should be the same for both plants.

Companions:
As per the redcurrant bush, with legumes for soil nutrition; sacrificial plants such as nasturtiums for attracting aphids and onion varieties for discouraging beetles and other plant pests.

Harvesting/Preserving:
Whitecurrants make excellent tasty jams and jellies, and although white in color the jams will turn out slightly pink. This is probably because the whitecurrant is actually an albino cultivar of the redcurrant.

Like the red and blackcurrant varieties they are harvested by cutting away the clumps and either freezing in bags or immediately turning into jams, jellies etc.

Recipes in the next section.

Jams Jelly's & Co

Jams and jellies, preserves and conserves have always been a great way to not only use up excess fruit production; but also to store it for later use and indeed to add another dimension to the larder and your recipe books!

When considering the recipes below remember that most of the fruits can be simply exchanged for others to get the different jams. In other words the same recipes will do many kinds of jams with the only difference being in the fruits used. Yes I know – kinda stating the obvious – but it has to be said…

General rules/Tips:

Testing readiness:
First of all place 2 or 3 saucers in the freezing compartment of the fridge to cool, before starting to make your jam. This way you can test if the jam is ready by putting a spoonful on a cold plate and placing the fridge for a few minutes.

After it has cooled then a crinkly skin should form on the surface; this can be tested with a gentle prod with your finger. If not, then boil for a further 5 minutes or so and test again on a fresh cold saucer.
Repeat until jam is ready to be jarred.

Storing/Jarring:
When storing in jars make sure that the jars and the lids have been boiled to sterilise them.

Place lids upside down on clean kitchen roll whilst they are waiting to be put on jars, and do not touch the inside of the lids otherwise you are likely to get mould forming on the top of your jam!

Pour jam into hot, dry jars to within ½ inch of the top, and place a disc of wax-proofed paper on top before screwing down the lid.

Berries:

Harder fruits like the currants are normally best boiled for a few minutes before adding the sugar, in order to soften them a little.

Softer fruits like raspberries or blackberries are usually best added at the same time as the sugar to make for the ideal consistency.

That said, here are some good recipes for you to consider.

Jam Recipes:

Strawberry Jam:

2 lbs strawberries
4 cups white sugar
¼ cup of lemon juice

After hulling the strawberries (removing the leaf part), crush the fruit in a large bowl until you have about 4 cups of mashed strawberries. Mix together with the lemon juice and sugar in a heavy bottomed pan and stir gently over a low heat until the sugar is all dissolved

Increase the heat, and bring the mixture to a full boil, stirring often. When the mixture reaches 220 degrees F (105 degrees C); transfer to hot sterile jars, leaving 1/4 to 1/2 inch headspace, and seal.

***

Gooseberry Jam:

2lbs Gooseberries
2lbs sugar
3/4 pint of water

After washing and trimming the berries, place in a heavy-bottomed saucepan with the water and bring to the boil for 1-2 minutes. Simmer for around 15 minutes further until the gooseberries are soft, add the sugar and boil for a further ten minutes or so.

Test the jam and store in hot jars as per previous guidelines.

***

Blackberry Jam:

2 cups blackberries
2 cups white sugar
Juice of one large lemon

Crush the raspberries in a large bowl and add the sugar and lemon juice. Mix thoroughly before adding the mix to a thick-bottomed saucepan and simmering on high heat for 5-10 minutes.

Reduce heat and simmer for a further 15 minutes, remove from the heat and test with the 'cold saucer' test, then jar if ready.

***

Blackcurrant Jam:

2lb blackcurrants
1 pint water
2 ½ lbs white sugar

Wash the berries thoroughly, and rinse in a colander; removing any stalks or leafy bits – along with any bad berries.

Add the berries and the water into a pan, then simmer for 10-15 minutes until the berries are soft. Add the sugar and make sure it is all dissolved, and then simmer for a further 15 minutes or so.

Scum may develop on the surface as the mixture is boiling; ignore this for the meantime but add a small knob of butter and stir well after mixture is away from the heat. This will remove most of it – scrape off the rest before pouring into jars.

Test using the saucer method described earlier, and boil longer if needed. Pour into your prepared jars and store.

***

Jelly's & Preserves:

Redcurrant Jelly:

2 lbs redcurrants
20oz white sugar
½ cup of water.

No need to separate the fruit. Just add the washed fruit, stems & all to the water, and bring slowly to the boil in a preserving pan.

Stir the mixture as it is boiling, pressing down on the fruit all the while to release the flavour. After about ten minutes add the sugar, then when it has dissolved completely bring to a fast boil for 8-9 minutes

Meanwhile place a muslin cloth inside a colander atop a suitable bowl, then pour in the liquid. If you do not mind a cloudy jelly then gently squeeze the fruit for more flavour, otherwise just let the mixture seep through.

Pour the strained liquid into sterilised jars as per jam recipes.

***

Strawberry & Redcurrant Preserve:

1 lb Hulled & quartered strawberries
1 lbs redcurrants
1 ½ lbs sugar

Juice of 1 lemon
1 tble spoon water.

After cleaning and de-stemming the fruit, add the whole mix to a suitable heavy-bottomed pot, and stir over a medium heat until the sugar has dissolved completely.

Turn up the heat and boil vigorously for 8-10 minutes, stirring gently. The fruit should be soft but not completely dissolved.

Test using the saucer method for setting ability and if needed bring back to the boil for a few minutes. When done pour into jars as per previous guidelines.

***

3 Berry Preserve:

½ lb blackberries:
½ lb blueberries
½ lb raspberries
½ cup of water
12 oz of sugar
Juice of 1 lemon

Put the whole mix into a pot and bring slowly to the boil for 5 minutes. Stir gently and boil on high heat for a further 8-10 minutes more.

Test a drop on a cold plate for consistency and setting ability. Put back on heat if need be, otherwise pour into hot, sterilized jars.

***

Blueberry Chutney:

3 cups fresh blueberries
1 tble spoon fresh ginger
1/3 cup apple cider vinegar
½ cup brown sugar
2 tble spoon cornstarch or cornflour
1 stick of cinnamon
1 small clove of garlic

Place all the ingredients in a suitable saucepan and bring to the boil for around 2-3 minutes. Remove the cinnamon stick and boil for further 10-15 minutes. Allow to cool before placing in a sealed airtight container, and storing in the fridge.
This should keep for up to two weeks.

***

Gooseberry Chutney:

1 cup cider vinegar
½ cup water
½ tsp salt
1 whole allspice
1 cinnamon stick
6 whole cloves
10 cups gooseberries
¼ tsp grated nutmeg

Add the brown sugar, water and salt to a heavy-bottomed pot. Tie together the allspice, cinnamon stick and cloves in a muslin bag and add to the mix.

Bring to the boil for about 5 minutes, then add the gooseberries and the nutmeg. Reduce heat and simmer for another 30 minutes or so until the mixture has thickened and the fruit is soft.

Remove the muslin bag, squeezing the juices back into the pot. Stir and pour the contents into hot sterilized jars as per jam recipes.

This will make around 8 jars of chutney.

***

Authors Note:

I do hope that you have found the guidelines laid out in this book to be both helpful and informative. I have always found that growing berries makes a great addition to my vegetable gardens, and will often grow low-lying vegetables or strawberries under the spaces occupied by the bushes.

This helps to increase my fruit & veg production without using more space, and greatly reduces my weeding efforts!

I have included some Companion Planting and Organic growing methods in this work, as I am particularly keen NOT to use artificial pesticides or fertilizers in my own gardens – there is simply no need to when an understanding of nature's own abundance is gained.

For a fuller explanation of Companion planting methods and organic gardening generally, I have included links to books that you may find of interest – shameless plug I know, but the bills have to be paid (wry smile!).

With berry bushes in particular, it is important to at least know the basics with regard to preserving, as the crop is often mostly ready at the same time. The jam and chutney recipes I have included here, just have to be altered slightly

to accommodate your berry production – don't be afraid to experiment and develop your own delicious recipes.

Finally - a huge thanks for purchasing this book, your support is appreciated. If you can spare the time, and have the inclination, a good honest review on Amazon would also be much appreciated.

Thanks again.

James

Relevant Books by Same Author

Raised Bed Gardening 5 Book Bundle

Raised Bed Gardening 3 Book Bundle

Companion Planting

Growing Berries

Square Foot Gardening

Square Foot Vs Raised Bed Gardening

Vegetable Gardening Basics

James Paris is an **Amazon Best Selling Author**, you can see the full range of books on his Amazon author page.

10519747R00039

Printed in Great Britain
by Amazon.co.uk, Ltd.,
Marston Gate.